BETWEEN THE DREAM

Edited by Shawn Jordan
Cover Design by Jen Marquez
Cover Photography by Chan C. Smith

Printed in the United States of America
CreateSpace, 2014
ISBN 978-1502313195

Join the Nation at www.unashamednation.com

Between the Dream

by Richard L. Taylor Jr.

Table of Contents

Page

Author's Note

You are not alone. Yes! I get it, the struggle is real. Many times in life you get to these plateaus and you hate where you are. Once you reach that plateau you feel like you will be stuck there forever. You've put in so much hard work, you've shed so many tears, you've tried to do everything right like everyone suggested; but you still find yourself staring hardship and despair in the face. A lot of times you sweep these feelings under the rug and try to go on your merry way as if nothing bothers you, but truth be told - you're dying inside.

You may be at a point in your life where you are either trying to complete school, starting a new job, pursuing a career or business opportunity, attempting to prove yourself on your school's team; or just trying to figure out your purpose in life. No matter where you are, please understand me when I say, "YOU ARE NOT ALONE!" You might be thinking, "Richard, you don't know me personally," and you would be right. What I do know is that you and I bleed the same blood, fear failure and work towards the same goal of a better life than what we were born into.

Beyond that, I understand where you are because I struggle with the feeling of being alone from time to time, specifically the past several months. I have been working hard to make my dreams become a reality, and I feel like the more I push, the more resistance comes. I'll be honest enough to tell you that as I was working to further my goals, I hit bad luck and rock bottom simultaneously. A few unfortunate mishaps and long period of no income had me facing eviction, repossession and struggling just to bring groceries in the house.

These kinds of struggles can play heavily on your psyche and make you feel like you want to give up on your dreams, your goals and yourself. I felt so alone during my hardship, like no one out there heard my cries. I kept asking myself, "Who motivates the motivators when they need to be motivated?" These are the times it seems like there is no one to turn to, and no one who truly understands just how deep your pain is. But, you are not alone.

I know the struggle is real, and I know how hard it is to keep moving in times like these. But with every step comes the opportunity to make another. As hard as it may be, this is the time when you have to sit back and assess everything that you are dealing with. Address your deeply-rooted pain and use that pain to push you through. In doing this myself, I recognized that pain produces three important traits that you will need to get you through. They are perseverance, character, and power.

You have to use your pain to push you past this temporary place in your life. Yes it may be hard, but IT IS doable. The primary reason you should push through it and shake it off is because you never know when your moment or opportunity will come. It may seem like nothing better is coming, but if you continue to work hard towards your goal, it's bound to happen. It happened for me and I know it can happen for you. It's just a matter of having the drive and desire to see your dreams become a reality.

I know that the road seems long, hard and unbearable, but you can and will make it. Appreciate the time that you have to yourself to evaluate your circumstances and figure out how to move forward. After you can identify your pain and be real with yourself, instead of sweeping things under the rug, let that pain be your guiding light. Trust me, it will work. If you think I'm lying, just reread this preface and remember that everything you read is from my own personal pain. Trust in your gift, trust in yourself, and trust in God. The struggle is real, but you are not alone.

Demise

One of the definitions of the word demise is, "the end or failure of an enterprise or institution." In this context, demise is the hindrance or sometimes downfall we are warned to steer away from. In my first book titled *Unashamed* I wrote, "The decisions you make in life determine your destiny and your demise." I use the term demise because I think that we as people can face ends and failures as well. I believe that the greatest gift we have been given is the power of choice. No matter what comes our way - good, bad or ugly - we control the decisions that we make. We live in a time where everything around us is based off of decisions. The economic crises, mass school shootings, taking a chance on love, graduating from college, etc. - all of these events are the result of someone's decision making.

In this book I discuss specific topics that can create cycles that lead to a person's demise. It is important to understand that the potential for your demise has and always will stem from the decisions you make. It has never been about being born into a bad situation or coming from a privileged or affluent upbringing. Demise is solely based on one's decision as an action or reaction to their current circumstance. In order for us as a people to live out our full destiny we must first understand how to avoid a lifestyle of demise due to lousy decision making. It's been said that "with every step comes the decision to make another." I believe in this statement and it is my hope that you understand that no matter where you are in life, you can make the changes you need to make in order to live the life you've always dreamt about.

My goal is to show you how to break certain cycles and help you to live a progressive and destined future.

Chapter 1: You Ain't Shit

"When they said you ain't shit, they were right; because you were never created to lack value."
- Richard L. Taylor Jr.

I know you looked at the title of this chapter and said, "Richard...really? This is how you choose to start your book? You have youth and teens who read your books, why would you put this in here?" Hold your horses...it's okay...trust me. About a month and a half ago, I was at a mentoring conference in Chicago. During this event there was a segment where the youth were encouraged to speak and what happened next really blew my mind. The conference organizers invited five attendees on stage to say one thing that they hate hearing from their parents or guardians. When one young man got his turn to speak, the words "you ain't shit, and you ain't never gone be shit" came out of his mouth. The audience gasped and moaned. You could feel the pain from both him and the audience as it circulated its way through the room. Even though the conference ended on a very high note, that young man's comment stuck with me for the next few days. It wasn't like this was the first time I had heard these comments. I have heard this said to my friends. I have even heard it said to me by people I love and care about.

The next week I spoke at my former high school and I decided to start with an icebreaker/experiment. I asked the students to stand if the question or comment I was about to say applied to them. The first two questions and/or comments weren't controversial. However, when I asked my final question and said "If someone has ever told you, 'You ain't gone be shit in life,' please stand or remain standing," the response was astounding. Not only did the room go silent, but the pain on the faces of the young men and women was evident and heartbreaking. I found the numbers staggering. I did this in five different classes with approximately 20 students in each engagement. The results were, between 7-8 students per class would stand or remain standing to admit that this type of comment was said to them. Some students laughed when they stood up, as if they had heard the phrase so many times, they had become completely numb to it. After leaving the school that day I could not get their faces out of my mind. I kept wondering how many more of the 7 billion people on this earth have been victims to this type of mental abuse. And of those who have heard it, how many walk around to this very day actually believing it? I was also taken back at the thought that this is arguably something that has been, and is presently being instilled into people at a very young age. One thing to know about me is that I'm all about being realistic, raw and uncut. The reality is that this is an epidemic that is growing in all communities, in many different languages. Allow me to say to you truthfully, honestly, and with all sincerity, "You ain't shit, and you ain't never gonna be shit!" Huh?!

We all know the word shit is a term created to describe fecal matter. But there is one particular definition of the word that I want to focus on, and that definition says shit is "something of little value or quality." Let's think about this. The fact is that you have a value that no one in this world can take away - no matter what they say, or how hard they try. This, my friend, is why I can honestly say you will never be the definition shit. You weren't born lacking quality or value. I know sometimes it may feel that way when you sit back and reflect on how eff'ed up your life is at times, or when you feel like your dreams aren't coming true fast enough. That feeling is completely normal. But a potential demise that comes with it is feeding the beliefs that "This shit is never going to work" or "Maybe they were right when they said, I ain't gone be shit." I'm sure you have heard the phrase "you are what you eat." This statement might seem cliché, but it is the honest to God truth. You are exactly what you feed yourself daily, both physically and mentally.

I remember putting on 170lbs during my first two years of college. From day one I went on a food frenzy that was out of control. I had a meal plan that gave me $110 worth of food each week, plus I had money in the bank. As I looked back, I realize there were specific things I ate that contributed to the massive amount of weight I gained. My diet consisted of junk and fast foods including whole pizzas, double cheeseburgers, Philly cheese steaks, sweets and suicide pops.

You're probably thinking "damn, that diet sucked," and you are right. But what sucked even more was the fact that I ate these things daily. When it came to my eating there was no such thing as moderation. I just ate and ate and ate and soon began to notice a change in my physical appearance and condition. I would have one popped pants button here, one ripped dress shirt there, one heavy breath after the next, and one sharp pain after another. These were signs that my decision about the food I choose to eat not only had an impact on my outer appearance, but was clearly having a negative impact on my health and livelihood.

I use this example, because our mouths and our thoughts are a lot alike. When we are attacked by our reality, we perceive things, we take in ideas, we digest them and let them settle and they become a part of our very being. Someone may have told you that you're worthless, you won't amount to anything, or that you're nothing. Or, maybe you were told you were going to be just like a person who was perceived negatively, with comment like, "You just like your no-good ass father or mother." Whatever negative comment you heard, you ingested. You can try to deny it all day long, but as much as you tried to suppress it, it still became a part of your belief system. I don't care how deep down inside you managed to suppress it, seeds from negative words were sown and you carry that weight around because it was so rigorously fed to you.

So now you are faced with a dilemma: "How do I get this dead weight off of me, Richard? How am I supposed to move on when I feel like my body will collapse at any moment? I have allowed myself to believe I won't amount to anything and now I have begun to act out what I thought of myself? The solution is as easy or as complicated as you allow it to be. DETOX! You must detoxify yourself permanently of the negative experiences and thinking that has helped create the dark hole you're in. When I first started working out and getting down to a manageable weight, I had to detox, or rid, my body of all of the poisonous substances that were causing me to be overweight. This is the same thing that you have to do mentally. You have to detoxify your mind and all of the negative things that were ever said or done to you. Yeah, I know this is hard to do, but like I said, it can be as easy or as hard as you make it.

I know sometimes it's hard to get over the malicious things that hurt you. But if you continue to hold on to something you claim you don't want, you may need to consider detoxifying yourself first. Detoxifying helps you to get rid of the mindset that makes it easy for you to hold on to and recycle all of the waste that has been thrown at you over the years. A few ways to detoxify yourself would be to use positive affirmations; and admitting and accepting the fact that you are human and not perfect. My personal favorite is to address the hurt and anguish head on, and realize that you have already overcome it. I say this, because if you hadn't you may not be alive right now. It is okay to remind yourself that you are stronger than the mental abuse that tries to control you.

Chapter 2: Perception

"Be thankful for what you have; you'll end up having more. If you concentrate on what you don't have, you will never, ever have enough."
- Oprah Winfrey

Sometimes during our process to our promise we are so focused on getting to the finish line that we forget to enjoy the journey. Now I'm sure that you are probably wondering how you can find joy in something that causes so much pain. Well, I believe that the ability to discern joy from pain is a matter of perspective. How you look at and perceive your situation is a key component to finding the joy in any situation.

In the previous chapter I wrote about the hardships that I faced while trying to get my career and first book off the ground. I complained tremendously during this time. There were plenty of times I felt like a joke and didn't understand why I had gotten started with this mess in the first place. I wasn't satisfied and I wanted more; I struggled daily with my thoughts and wondered if this would ever amount to anything. I remember complaining and nagging to my wife and best friends over every little detail.

What I didn't realize was that I was rehearsing my problems and setting myself up for failure. Failure? Yes, failure! I was setting myself up for failure because I wasn't giving myself a chance to see the full perspective. I was too busy thinking and seeing my life in parts, instead of thinking about the bigger picture. I think at times we all get to this place where our perception of our situation causes us to misjudge where we are versus exactly where we are headed.

Growing up I never understood the whole "glass half empty, half full" analogy. As I got older it started to make much more sense. A lot of times we are plagued by the "reality" of situation and this can keep us from moving forward and excelling more. We can get to a place where we try to predicate our outcome simply based on where we currently are. We will spend so much time describing our problems to friends and family, or anyone who will listen; instead of putting our head, heart and energy into discovering a solution. It's easy to identify our problems. But it will seem very hard to fathom just one solution. Yet what do you think would happen, if we alter our thought process and see our problems from a different lens?

No matter how bad your situation is, there's always a way to escape. It is up to you to find it. This is the beauty of personal growth. Consider some of today's leaders. If you read their bios or heard them speak, you would hear of many trials and tribulations they faced before reaching their goals. You'd see that there is a common theme when they talk about overcoming their problems. It all starts with perception. They didn't "pity party" their way to the top. Successful people actually spend time looking at their problems differently. Not only do they look at them differently, but they take the time to clear out the confusion around them by focusing on the strengths they have within. For a lot of them it was as simple as thinking back to a time when they faced adversity and how they overcame it.

In order to overcome adversity, you have to realize that many of the problems you experience are recycled tests given in different formats. Think about when you were in school. You would take weekly quizzes, and what would happen about two to four weeks later? You'd have a big test, and the exact same questions that were on the weekly quizzes would be on the test. Essentially, life is the same way. You should treat these life tests as though they are nothing new. Often times, you are being challenged by the exact same test you've experienced before, just in a different form. The people might be different, the struggle you face might have a different face, but the root of the problem may very well be something you have dealt with before. You have to get to a point where you say to yourself "enough is enough!" Perceive yourself as a victor before going into battle. Believe deep down inside that you can face whatever it is, and you can also conquer it! Try not to make excuses for yourself, and have a willingness to change your perception on your life and your situation.

I'm reminded of a quote that says, "The man that believes he can and the man that believes he can't are both normally right." So my question to you is - where do you stand in what you believe about yourself? Truth be told we can all avoid a life of demise. However that is determined by our decisions and our decisions are an exact reflection of our perception.

Chapter 3: Inadequacy

"Our deepest fear is not that we are inadequate. Our deepest fear is that we are powerful beyond measure."

- Marriane Williamson

I remember having a conversation with a friend about their previous and current employment situations. While they were grateful to have a job, they asked me, "Is it wrong that I want more out of life?" He reiterated more specifically, "Is it wrong that I don't want to work for somebody else?" They went on to explain how the jobs they had, made them feel a certain type of way. He said that having to sit and watch others as they came in and out of the workplace, and watching management treat lower workers as if they don't matter, can take a huge toll on a person's perception of themselves.

That feeling he had been feeling for some time is the same feeling many of us have dealt with or might even be dealing with now. It's the feeling of inadequacy. Inadequacy is just like a blood sucking leach. It clamps on to you in hidden places and secretly begins making its home. Inadequacy starts to feed on your areas of strength similar to a leach and makes you feel weaker and weaker, leaving you with overwhelming feelings of nothingness.

I explained to my friend that it's okay to want to work for yourself and want more out of life. I encouraged him to follow the passion he has to build his own business, but while he is doing that to remember those feelings of inadequacy. I told him to remember how he has been treated so that when it's his time to step into greater heights he can use his situation to be a better influence to and for those who believe in his vision. It's the exact same for you my dear friend. A lot of us didn't come from privilege and there was an immense amount of hard work and struggle we have to endure. So when your opportunity comes to attain greater positions, new leadership and every bit of elevation you can think of; you can be the change you have always wanted to see in the people around you.

Feelings of inadequacy can hinder you from being successful in your career, relationships, friendships, self-image and everything else in between. Even as you read this chapter, you might be reminded of your own areas of inadequacy, or you could be living a full-fledged inadequate life. When it boils down to it, inadequacy is just a mindset. It does not define the real you, the person who was created with a purpose in life. The person who has potential way beyond what anyone can imagine.

In a conversation with another friend we also discussed that people will look at you, judge you, and make preconceived notions about you, but their opinion doesn't mean a hill of beans in the grand scheme of things. A lot of us who are living life outside of the norm or taking unconventional routes to reach our goals will also experience these feelings from time to time, but it's all a part of the growth process. I believe it's important for us not to forget the humble beginnings. This way when we accomplish our goals or make it big, we can be reminded of not only what it took to get there, but also to extend love, compassion and care to the people we come in contact with.

Inadequacy is a disease that can taint your perception about yourself in a moment's notice. When you are facing struggles and you begin to have those feelings you must learn to understand that the struggle isn't about you, but is to be used as a testament to the people around you. For example, growing up I dealt with major depression. I always felt that I was alone in my journey with depression. However, studies from The National Institute of Mental Health have shown that approximately 14.8 million American adults have major depressive disorder. After I was able to overcome my depression and openly talk about it, I noticed an influx of people coming to share their stories with me. By the end of these conversations they would say things like "If it wasn't for you sharing your story with me, I would have killed myself" or "Thank you for giving me courage to speak up and seek help." Moments like these revealed the bigger picture to me. I realized that this journey we call life is so much bigger than what we can fathom. People not only need our stories, but they also need our love and help as well. They need you. I am constantly reminded that we are put in hellacious situations so that someone else doesn't have to be. We live in such a self-indulgent society that we can forget that a lot of the stuff we go through can be used for us to be a blessing to another person in need. Now that you know people can benefit from hearing your stories of feeling inadequate, it's time for you to address your personal feelings toward it to move forward. I understand that feelings of inadequacy might not come from work, but maybe a relationship or a person's physical appearance. Feelings of inadequacy can also come from the fact that you may think and speak differently from the next person. It could come from negative comments heard from parents or teachers as you were growing up. As I discussed in Chapter 1, you might have heard people tell you that you are going to be a screw up just like your mother or father, or that you won't amount to anything when you get older comparing you to a sibling, cousin or a friend. It's possible you heard that you didn't fit in with the "in" crowds. No matter what was said to you or how painful it is to think about, at the end of the day you have the choice to make those inadequate words adequate in your life.

Here is the one action step I want you to take when dealing with feelings of inadequacy. TAKE CONTROL! Understand and believe that you are the only person who has control over you. Therefore, if anything is said or done to you that might cause these feelings, remember that the words and actions of others can only be solidified with your approval. Believe it or not, no matter how low you feel, you still have full control over how you deal with everything that comes your way. You simply have to believe you have the control over yourself to respond and react in a way that will create better outcome. A lot of times we get the impression that our lives are just too far gone, when really we have just lost a sense of power. The power to overcome every obstacle that life throws at you - it has always been there. Think back to a time in your life when you were even the least bit strong, and in that moment you will pin point your power. A lot of time people will seek external motivation, but the true answers and truth to who you are and the power you have has and always will reside in you. I encourage you to find your power to fight off those feelings of inadequacy and take control of your thoughts and how you respond.

Chapter 4: The New Suicide

"In the end one needs more courage
to live than to kill himself."
- Albert Camus

There is a famous song that says "after you've done all you can, you just stand." I love this saying, because I believe it speaks to the life of so many people who are in the process of or have chased their dreams at one point and time. Think about it this way; you've put in so much hard work and dedication into pursuing your dreams and at times you probably feel like it's not worth going any farther. At times it might feel as though your results will never change, and that you will only receive the minimum output after putting in the maximum amount of energy and time. You may possibly feel like everything you have done up until this point was a fluke or in vein. But hear me clearly when I say that you are so much closer than you think. Trust me when I tell you - you are on what many would call the road "less" traveled. Personally I don't believe that name does this process any justice. This long drawn out journey of life is a road traveled by many, but only survived by few because they were strong and courageous enough to keep moving forward without throwing in the towel. It has been my experience that the road "less" traveled is really a weeding out process. Over the past two years I have found that there is not much separation from those who experience immense success and those who live a complacent life. That it is their mental take away of the situation at hand, how it affects their overall self-esteem and how they choose to respond through their determination that makes the difference. You can take Oprah for example and how while working to create a platform for herself, she was constantly told that she didn't have the look or face for TV. However she worked harder throughout her career and was determined to prove to herself that she could be what she believed she could be. I believe that her current success speaks for itself. What if Oprah believed what she was told instead? Unfortunately, you have people who do fall into that a negative belief of themselves after someone tears them down. Some people have all the talent in the world, but will give up after being criticized and talked about. The pain was too much, the work was too hard, or sometimes they just feel like all hope is lost.

This is what I like to call the "new suicide." Typically when you hear about suicide, it's always from the stand point of a person trying to physically harm themselves. This new suicide is much different; everything about it is geared towards your dreams, vision and goals. You don't physically harm yourself, but you can still harm yourself by simply doing nothing. If you take a look back, everything that I have discussed in the first three chapters can all lead to the new suicide. Negative words spoken against you, having a negative perception of ourselves or our situation, or the feeling of inadequacy and not being good enough are all actions that can lead to the new suicide. These thoughts and feelings cause a very difficult road block and our response to that road block determines whether we decide to live and push forward towards our goals; or just exist and allow the problems to overtake us and become complacent by doing nothing. The new suicide is based on a person giving up in the greatest areas of their life, and being totally okay with it. The new suicide is giving up on your dreams and your future when the going gets tough or never pursuing your dreams at all.

I remember speaking at the Council for Opportunity in Education National Conference in 2013 and kicking off the session with an ice breaker. I asked five questions and the last two were about things that would be a lot more personal and hard for people to deal with. The questions were related to suicide, and not many people were standing when I asked about attempting or contemplating it. When I stated to them that everyone has done it, they looked stunned. "How dare you call me a liar," was the look that came across many of their faces. As I explained further, I could tell that it began to make more sense to the audience; that the thought and action of suicide is not always a physical battle. It has been my experience through my work that I see people discussing how they have thoughts of wanting to quit or walk away more than they have about wanting to physically kill themselves. In life, specifically when things get hard, we will deal with tricks of the mind that seem real. They can be from past words, hurts, or failures. Or they might be coming from people or situations that are current in our lives. You might be feeling like you should give up, or that a specific individual was right about how your lack of talent or skill. My message for you here is don't allow the tricks of your mind make you feel like some kind of failure who should just give up. In life, you are going to face some messed up situations and you will feel like you've been dealt a few bad hands, but understand - that is normal.

In my first book "Unashamed," I discussed my personal battle with suicide that occurred between the ages of 10 and 20. My experience with depression and suicide felt like an on again off again relationship, or so I thought. After I finally decided to take back the little bit of life I felt I had at the time, I began to notice a lot of things about myself. One thing in particular was that the action of suicide was always within me, but it first needed to be triggered by my thoughts. There is a passage in the Bible from proverbs 23:7 that says "As a man thinks, so is he." The reason why the action of committing suicide was so easy for me was because the thought itself was invoked. Everything was controlled by my thoughts and my thoughts were always triggered by the negative things that were happening around me. Every fight with my parents, every argument with the girl I was dating, every pound of weight I gained, and every bad grade I received in class; they all triggered the thoughts that led me to constant suicide attempts.

Now let's fast forward to the present and take a look at our personal situations. We will get hit with trials and disappointments as we're working towards our dreams and goals. It is those dark hours that can change our outlook on life, and once our outlook is changed we can't help but to view things as being "all bad." If you personally haven't witnessed the "all bad" mentality in your life, I can almost guarantee that you can spot it in the lives of someone else you know. Think I'm lying? Just think of that one Facebook friend that is always online complaining about how things will never work out. You know the one that you are almost certain you will see a negative post from every time you log in? In all seriousness that "all bad" mentality is a key thought that leads us to acting out exactly what we think.

After spending time in the hospital for my final suicide attempt, I was faced with the doubt that I could ever recover mentally. The thoughts of suicide were still there, because I still had thoughts of lack, inadequacy and rejection about myself. Furthermore, I lacked the strength that I needed to fight off the negative thoughts and words coming my way. I came to the conclusion that in order to heal my hurting heart, I would need to do some soul searching and stop attempting mental suicide on myself. In order for me to fight off this new suicide in my mind, I had to shift my focus from my problems to myself. I had to do some soul searching to find some kind of good in myself that could help me combat against all of the negativity I felt towards my purpose. A lot of times when we think about soul searching we think about finding out all of our likes and dislikes. What makes us comfortable and what makes us tick, but this is not what I mean. I quickly found out that soul searching comes in the form of investing or re-investing positive thoughts and affirmations into back into self.

This is the same approach we need to take in our personal lives. In order to heal you must properly invest or re-invest into yourself. It is important to be sure that whatever you decide to invest has the power to bring you beneficial gain. So if you have to use post-it notes with words of affirmation and stick them up around your house then do it. Just make sure the words you post are beneficial. If you need to be around friends make sure that they are investing beneficial attributes into your self-esteem. The reason I say this is because every friend does not want to see you succeed in life.

No matter the investment, you have to be willing to take the time to understand what areas of your life you are investing in, and what proper investments you need to make in order for you to be your best. If you choose not to invest or invest the wrong things then the chances of you repeating the cycle of the mental suicide are very high. Be willing to take the time you need, use your God given talent and wisdom to make your investment work for you. Whatever you do, don't be cheap on yourself when it comes to what you invest within yourself, your dreams and goals. If you are going to fight off mental suicide and the thoughts that create it, you have to do so with positive thoughts and actions strong enough to combat it. Be willing to put the maximum investment into your mental stability and your self-esteem. When you do this you will begin to not only see a difference, but easily fight off the mental distractions that cause the new suicide.

Chapter 5: Idle Time

"The proper function of man is to live, not to exist. I shall not waste my days in trying to prolong them. I shall use my time."
– Jack London

There are a few things in life that you can never get back. The biggest for me is TIME. No matter how you wished you would-of, should-of or could-of spent time passed; you can't change it once it's gone. When working towards your goals in life how you spend your time is crucial. Now, as a disclaimer I am all about balance in life. However I believe that people sometimes use balance as an excuse or for good reasoning. Have you ever seen a person who has all of these big dreams, but all they ever do is talk about them? When it's time to work towards their goals they always have an excuse talking about everything else they are doing in their life, and how they don't have time or the need to keep the balance in their life? We have been given 86,400 seconds in each day and how we spend that time makes all the difference. When I first started my business I made it a goal to study successful business people and entrepreneurs and I notice a trend. They were all very strategic in their daily time structure. No matter what they had to do that day, they were committed to it and made no excuse for it not to be done. Author Frank Ra stated that "time is the ultimate currency." He says that every day we each have 86,400 seconds as a gift of life, and when the day finishes, any unused time is gone. If you are going to be successful in whatever it is you love, you have to think of time as money. This is a concept that is learned by few and mastered by even fewer.

When you have a goal and you are truly locked in on it, you will begin to do whatever it takes to see it come to pass. I decided to give this structured time theory a chance and when I did I noticed a drastic change. People typically ask me now, how have I been able to speak and present at big events and venues at the age of 26. I attribute a lot of that to how I started spending my idle time. I knew that I wanted to push the envelope in my career and execute every goal when I was 23. I saw it happen for others my age and even younger. So I said to myself, "Why not me?" I began to sacrifice some old ways and bad habits. I stopped giving so much time to the television and pointless social media browsing after realizing just how distracting it had become.

During my time in college I used to watch a lot of reality TV. Even though I knew that these shows weren't real, one real thing kept sticking out to me. This was that I was playing a major role in making perpetrators a lot of money. I seriously had to sit back and think to myself "How am I going to be where I want in a few years, by sitting on my butt watching other people live life?" Too many times we get caught up in a fantasy world created by someone else, while trying to escape our own reality.

The truth is, no matter where you've come from, the fantasy or dream life that you sit back and adore could ultimately be your reality. It all starts with shifting your actions and your approach to spending your idle time. It is important for you to realize that how you spend your idle time will determine your success. For me, it was almost as if I saw myself 20 years from now still watching shows talking about "I wish that was me." So, I began to substitute TV and foolish social media for entertainment with reading, writing and studying my craft. I would read books on time management, self-help books on personal growth and even inspirational articles online that I would see friends post. My reading began to help me expand my writing and speaking. I gain a lot of knowledge from other great leaders' work.

During this time I discovered that anything in life is available to you and anything is possible, but how you spend your idle time will determine your success in real life. You have to make a conscious decision to stop being controlled by the things you love to do but waste your time. Everybody's struggle is different but we all have certain "kill factors" that keep us distracted. I can't begin to tell you how many people have brilliant ideas, but lack the concentration, motivation, and drive to actually see their plans become reality. People are so easily distracted by games, TV, people, and a million other things that they have absolutely no significance in setting themselves up to prosper in the future. Sometimes we have the tendency to ignore our priorities because we are distracted by kill factors.

In order for you to change how you spend your idle time, you need to do two important things. You first have to be honest with yourself and identify your "time killers." Ask yourself, "What are the things I do that distract me from maximizing my 86,400 seconds each day?" Are you hanging out on social media for hours at a time? Do you find yourself watching all the latest videos on WorldStar.com? If you're playing video games, how many hours a day do you devote to it? Or maybe you like watching someone else audition their God given talents on TV? Whatever it is, be honest and ask yourself, "Is this really helping me move forward with my goals in life?" Chances are they are not. If it's not helping you then it is just a temporary fix. A temporary fix that is setting you up to stay in permanent confinement, and keep you occupied from pursuing your dreams. Sometimes even keeping you focused more on the distractions than the goals. I encourage you to identify what areas you might feel are time killers and distractions for you and be willing to let them go.

Once you have identified your time killers, the second step is for you to replace them with the goals you want to accomplish in your life. Despite what we've been told, good things don't just come to those who wait. Good things come to those who put the work in their craft before they ever physically reach the goal they have in mind. So if you are really going to see success in your life, then it's time to start viewing your time as money and determine where and how your 86,400 seconds can be spent more effectively. Re-investing the proper attention into your idle time will begin to show you greater return then you could ever imagine.

Chapter 6: Waiting On Your Moment

"I'm tired of living day to day like everything's
alright. As long as I stay hustling I'm gone shine.
I'm just waiting on my moment."

- Jeremiah

I can recall so many times hearing my
elders refer to the people of the 21st century as
a "microwave generation." They talked about
how we are always in a rush for everything
without "paying our dues." I used to think that it
was the dumbest saying in the world, but over
time it began to make more and more sense to
me. Now-a-days it seems like everything we
work for is expected right away. There seems to
be a loss of time and appreciation when it comes
to attaining goals and accomplishments. We live
in a world that is so fast paced; we tend to forget

to prepare for what's important and beneficial to our future. I've realized that if we want to avoid a life of demise, then preparation and patience in our craft better be our best friend.

I remember at the start of my career as a speaker, I had to do all of the ground work myself. I was literally a one man army handling cold calls, emails, and doing all of my own marketing and publicity. This is by no means a complaint; however this is what I had to do in order to get my career off the ground. After getting several hundreds of "No's," I finally encountered a few who said yes. Once I did get an invitation to speak, I would then think, "Oh crap, I don't have a speech fully prepared." I had gotten so used to waiting on my moment, that I hadn't taken the time to prepare for something dynamic. What I was really doing was limiting myself from reaching my full potential by not being prepared for what I always wanted. I began to realize that I had become a victim to excuses and good reasoning. Reasoning as to why I hadn't prepared properly, and reasoning that led to justification of why it was okay to not be prepared for an opportunity that might only come once in a lifetime. I would try to make myself feel better by saying "Oh I'm already gifted and have a way with words…I'll be fine." I know a lot of us have done this. Whether it is while in school preparing for a last minute exam or paper, writing a proposal for work, or not properly preparing before a sporting event.

The truth is, when we continue to not properly manage our time and neglect to prepare for pivotal moments which can carry us to our goals, we will always be our own worst enemy. Your moment can come at any time and it's up to you to be ready to attack and seize the moment. That moment might not come instantaneously, but you have to work as if it will come in an instant. Your journey to success is not going to be like pulling up in the drive thru at McDonalds, Burger King or your favorite fast food restaurant.

Your journey is one that requires perseverance, determination and an immense amount of patience. Patience more than anything else will be your best friend, and a concept that will help you at times when the anxiety from waiting starts to creep up on you. In today's fast paced world, it seems we have lost the value of what it means to be patient and it has caused major confusion for the up and coming generations. A lot of times we get overly excited about where we are headed and we expect things to come instantaneously just after a little bit of work. Despite what we see in the mass media, the majority of us will not be YouTube sensations and blow up off of one hit video going viral.

It appears that it's easy for us to get caught up in our desires to reach our goal and never enjoy the present moment. The reality is that many of us spend our lives trying to make it big that we forget to connect with the present moment. We seem to be expecting to become happy in the future to the point where it can feel like the future will never come. Always be sure to pay attention to your experience in the present moment.

So what exactly am I saying to you? It's simple, be careful not to rush through life trying to get to your big moment and not embracing what seems hard to overcome in your road to making you better. When we are in between the dream, it is hard to accept the current situations that have been placed in front of us. Yeah I get it, sometimes the pain is hard to deal with or some days we just want to hide in a hole, and that's cool. But you have to get to a point where you can shake those feelings and stop fast forwarding your way through life.

If you really want success or just more out of your situation you have to start being intentional with everything you do. Whether it's how you schedule your day to day time, preparing for an upcoming event or big job interview; whatever it might be, start being more intentional about how you pursue those things. Otherwise, you will find yourself skipping your way through every important moment and waving goodbye to precious opportunities. Now I'm no psychic, and I'm not exactly sure where you are in your life right now. But I do know, in life you always have another chance to get it right.

Chapter 7: Solitude

"Solitude gives birth to the originality in us, to the beauty unfamiliar and perilous - to the poetry. But also, it gives birth to the opposite: to the perverse, the illicit, the absurd."
- Thomas Mann

Sometimes during your process you will feel completely alone. When I say alone, I mean ALONE. This includes separation from friends, family and everyone else that holds a spot close to your heart. The sense of loneliness might not always be a physical one. You will sometimes be overcome by the thoughts of loneliness even though you're surrounded by everyone that you love. This is a real and sometimes painful reality in your journey of life. I can recall plenty of times when I was with friends, visiting with family or spending time with my wife, and still having that feeling of being completely alone in my thoughts and ways.

I'm here to tell you that while you may feel alone at times in these specific instances, YOU ARE. In order to change that negative feeling, you must learn how to properly use that time to make yourself better in your craft, and more importantly as a person. An idle mind can lead you to demise quicker than anything else. This is because you are opening yourself up to all the wrong possibilities. Just because you may feel alone, doesn't mean that you can't be successful in accomplishing your dreams. Feelings of loneliness can actually be a great thing depending on how you respond to your situation.

I remember being at the brink of what I thought was going to be my defeat. My life was in complete and utter chaos. My wife had lost her job, my career wasn't fully taking off, and we were behind on our bills which was nothing new. But this time it was to the extreme. I had worked so hard the two months after my wife had been let go and I was seeking work everywhere. It was so bad that I actually began to call it quits and go back to the corporate world. Even though I didn't actually go back into the corporate world, I felt like my efforts to follow my dream were meaningless. What I didn't realize was that I was allowing my situation to make me feel this way. Between our credit debts, the car note being three months behind and on the repo list, and facing eviction, my back was against the wall.

I was so upset because I felt I had done everything in my power, from working small side jobs, to doing house cleaning and working almost for free. It was single handedly the most embarrassing time of my life. My wife and I had to go to food pantries because we had absolutely no money for groceries or link. Seriously, we couldn't afford to purchase link. I felt like such a failure, not as a leader, but as the leader of my home, as a husband. And now I was at a point where I was sitting at my lowest point the day before the bill collectors and land lord came to empty me out, and the only thing I felt was loneliness.

I had felt the feeling of loneliness plenty of times before, but never to this magnitude. I was in so much pain and misery. I was contemplating calling everything quits including my business goals, my desire to help other people, and even my marriage. Nothing seemed to make sense to me, and I kept asking myself "Why I chose to be different." Why did I choose to believe and where are all of those supporters during my darkest hour? As I sat there with my thoughts beating me down and making me feel worthless, I began to swell up fighting back tears. My brain felt like the YouTube search engine with so many things popping up at once. I cried and cried, and even began to question God on why I would never amount to anything. I then began to think back to a video I was listening to on my run earlier that day. The guy speaking said "Pain is temporary, it may last a day, a week, an hour or even a year, but eventually it will subside."

As those words played through my head, I began to tell myself, "This too shall pass." Yes I might feel alone, but how will I use this time of solitude to become a better person from this? How could I take the pain that I'm feeling now and keep moving forward? So I grabbed my iPhone and I began to type and type. I began to spew out every thought and feeling that I had until I began to write this chapter. Now I don't want you to get it confused when I say you are alone. Yes there are people out here going through similar circumstances and feel the same way you do. In that regard you are not alone. However as it relates to you being in a place of solitude dealing with your personal feelings and circumstance, you are alone. But that doesn't mean that it's a bad thing at all. Solitude is something that can actually be a great help during our journey. During my time of solitude and reflection, I began to write down my thoughts and I felt better. But what really got to me was reading what I had written down. After looking at my words and realizing how negative I sound, I couldn't help but to think that this is not me. In this moment, I began to get some clarity about myself and my situation. It dawned on me that I was becoming a victim to my own thoughts due to my negative outlook in a lonely moment.

I realized that in the process of thinking in our lonesome state we have the choice of either being victims or being victorious - even if we don't see the victory right away. I'm pretty sure a lot of you have similar thoughts and feelings during your hard times as well. You probably have a laundry list of emotions and feelings you could choose from. While I was able to pick from a positive thought even in a negative moment, not everyone would be able do the same thing. My urge for you is to find the smallest bit of light in your darkest hour. It might come through a song, video, book, or quote. Nonetheless, seek to find something that will shine a light on your situation.

After you do this, I encourage you to use your time alone to begin to break down your craft and the possibilities within. After all, it is your job to be the best you that you can be in whatever it is that you do best. My advice for you is that you take the pain that you feel in the loneliest of times and create something great out of it. Reflecting back on the concept of perception from chapter three about; don't look at a state of loneliness as something pitiful. Remember, your thoughts have the power to take you to the wrong extreme. Instead of using your energy to be upset about where you are and how messed up things seem, convert that energy and use your pain as motivation to do better. This is a craft that I have had to learn over the past year. Every time I feel some type of way about where I think I should be, or how much better things could be, I don't allow that pain the opportunity to create pity. Instead I treat my thoughts like a boxing match. I tell myself that I might be hurt, bruised or even down right tired, but that I still have life in me to throw another punch. And since I don't want to keep feeling that same pain, I try to throw punches back that will inflict as much pain on the problem - aka the knockout punch!

Every time I fight back and use my pain as motivation I begin to feel better. After I land that knockout punch on a particular problem, I take more time to focus on the ups and down from that battle, and analyze where I could be better the next time around. I realize that even in times of pain and hurt, I am still allowing character build within me. However, it important to note that once again, how I respond to that situation determines the kind of character - good or bad. No matter where you are right now, I encourage you to be bold and throw more punches, even while you are in pain. Yes you might be hurting and it feels like it's harder to move, but keep swinging back at your problems and understand that just because you are fighting the problem in solitude, doesn't make you weaker. It's just teaching you how to manage at times when you won't have people around you. Our friends can't always be there for us during our personal battles, but that doesn't make us any weaker, and it doesn't mean they love us any less. Just like in a boxer's corner, your team (the people who need your story and your help) are cheering you on waiting for your victory to help inspire theirs. Even in your darkest hour, keep swinging.

Chapter 8: Stop Fighting Closed Doors

"Don't allow the rejection from a closed door
of your good to distract you from opening the
door of your great".
- Richard L. Taylor Jr.

No matter where we are in life we will always be faced with things that come to an end: friendships, relationships, jobs, business and so on. I like to call these endings "closed doors." They represent leaving out of one space and going into another. The term "closed doors" has been used to describe the former things and people in a person's life. Sometimes these are doors that we have been waiting to close, but other times they are doors that close unexpectedly. When we have doors that close without any warning it can mess our entire world up; especially when we have a strong attachment to or love for whatever is behind the metaphoric door.

It is our human nature to fight and tug at the knob trying to reopen that door. We will make up excuses and say, "Oh I need closure," or believe that what rest behind that door was meant for us. We find ourselves trying everything we can to get that door open and it seems like nothing is working. The pain will seem to intensify as we think about the time, money and love we put into the person or thing behind the door. Finally, we'll try to convince ourselves that what is behind that door was something as good, and we may never experience it that again. If any of this sounds familiar, please allow me to stop you right there. You have to be careful not to get what was once good and now behind the closed door confused with the greatness that is to come.

A close friend shared with me how she was blessed to find a job not too long after graduating from college. She was very adamant about starting her job and doing her best so the employer could see her hard work and diligence, and see how valuable she was to the company. From the start of her first day she came out on fire. She was being her regular self and brining major help to a cluttered and frustrated office. She began to get compliments on how well she does her job and how she has so much potential. After about two weeks later, one of her direct bosses ended up leaving and taking a position outside of the state. My friend knew that she wasn't in a hurry to move up, but she did her best to help fill in the gap with the new missing link. Her work began to shine even more during this time and she began to catch the eye of some of the heads of the company. This was really exciting news to her, but she tried to remain humble and do her job. After four months, her other direct supervisor took another position and she was left to basically fend for herself. During this process she did not disappoint. She got even better with her job and proved that she could handle the responsibility.

Just as things seemed to be going in the right path she got word that the company was going to be letting her go and replacing her with her understudy. She was heartbroken. She went home in tears that day frustrated that she had put everything into this seemingly great opportunity and still got the short end of the stick. She vented to her friends about how she had put so much of her talent and skill into trying to make this company look good, all the while they were clearly sinking. She dealt with rude, inconsiderate and sometimes prejudices from people, yet kept a smile on her face through it all trying to be the bigger person.

She explained how she kept thinking in her head "This is mine," "It's supposed to be for me," "I won't find anything better than this." She was determined to do everything she could to prove herself in a place that was clearly moving in a different direction. As we talked, she recalled how during that time she was constantly putting all of her energy into a door that was closed. She admitted being so focused on fighting to keep that door open; at the time she didn't realize she was missing out on greater opportunities. She has since successfully launched her own business and programs, and doing pretty well for herself. She realizes that it would not have been like this had she still been tugging on that door of the past. Needless to say, I was intrigued to know what got her to stop fighting the closing door. She explained that she took her eyes off of her current situation and started to pay attention to other opportunities that were passing her up. She finally got to a point where she realized she was putting too much energy into something that was no longer worth her time. We have to look at our closed doors the same way. While some things are more permanent, there will be certain situations that are meant to be a means to an end - or seasonal opportunities.

If you are currently fighting with a closed door, or find yourself fighting with one in the future, my advice to you is to take your hand off the knob, stop trying to re-open the door, and breathe. Give yourself a moment to take it all in. When I say take it all in, I'm not just referring to the closed door, but to the future ahead of you as well. Focus on the bigger picture and ask yourself how much time is being wasted tugging at that person, place or thing that has ended. After you have given yourself adequate amount of time to really think things through, begin to shift your energy from the closed door to the opportunities waiting for you to respond. A lot of times we think that we have to start over, or do this whole clean slate thing. Honestly, the purpose of a means to an end is for you to take what you need to grow, and learn for your next level of greatness. So don't look at the closed door as a bad thing, because it can be used as a lesson learned for the future.

We can never know what that lesson is if we are still looking back, and trying to kick down an old door. My friend was very blessed in being able to catch herself before losing her way and becoming consumed with her closed door. On the contrary, I have seen some promising people forfeit great opportunity because they were too comfortable with what used to be. After you have taken everything in, addressed your new opportunities and converted your energy, my final bit of advice is to be prepared to repeat this process in due time. It might come sooner or it might come later, but it will surely come.

Shift your way of thinking about the closed doors to revolving doors. When you look at a revolving door notice how it continues to go in the same motion as people go through it. Revolving doors repeat a daily non-stop cycle. Our journey to reaching our dreams will prove itself to be the same way. Every time the door begins to move and shift you out of one place, accept the reality that the revolving door is really just you evolving to the next step. You're not losing the best opportunity of your life; you're not going to be worthless now that he or she is gone. You are actually going to be so much better, because now you know what you do and don't deserve. Your experiences are building your character and standards, whether you know it or not. So don't be a hindrance to yourself by having a closed door mentality. Your evolution is wrapped up in your revolution.

Chapter 9: Starve the Beast

"Starve the beast or be its feast."

- Richard L. Taylor Jr.

No matter how great our gift is, or how successful we become because of it, we are all plagued with a beast. Now when I say beast, I'm not talking about some type of mythical creature that we transform into when the clock strikes twelve. The beast I am referring to is a creature created that distracts and deters you away from being the best you can possibly be. The beast can be a multitude of things like a relationship, laziness, doubt, self-pity, anxiety, selfishness, conceitedness, and so on. It might not show its face often, but when it comes, it can destroy everything in its path. And even though the thought of this beast is deadly, we sometimes attach ourselves to it, giving it the power it needs to release carnage in our lives. Have you ever dealt with one thing in your life that you felt like you could never seem to shake or overcome? That one thing that has been bothering you since you were young and has somehow stayed stuck to you now in your latter years.

While we are caught up in the moment of dealing with our beast, it can seem so minimal. What we don't think about during those moments however, is that this beast is pulling us into a deeper and darker hole every time we engage with it. There is a passage in one of my favorite books, the Bible, which describes the beast as something created to steal, kill or destroy. Whatever your beast is, I encourage you to look at it the same way. Even though it seems like your beast is giving you comfort, it is really stealing your valuable time, killing your attention and quietly destroying your will to be your best self. Typically we don't acknowledge our beast for what it is until it's too late.

Have you ever just stopped, sat back and thought why am I struggling so hard with this problem, or why is it that every time I try to leave it alone it still has a way to come back and bother me? I've put some major thought into this, as this is something that I have personally struggled with. As I stated earlier in this chapter, everyone's beast looks different to them. I think back to my beast and how it was damaging me and the relationships around me. As a married man or men in general we don't usually discuss the underlying issues or struggles we face, but the reality is we need to. My beast came in the form of pornography and masturbation. Too honest? No, and here's why. Too many times the things that we are afraid to discuss are the same things that will break a lot of the ugly cycles that we are facing in our personal lives. An ugly cycle can be things such as, alcohol and drug abuse, physical and emotional abuse, lack of education and self-awareness, low self-esteem, and mental illness. While many will look at these issues from the outside and cast judgment, it's important to understand that there is always a root cause to the cycles we face. If we are really going to be selfless for others it is important to truly understand their personal struggles and not just what we perceive things to be.

My personal struggle was with pornography and masturbation for a very long time, to be exact since I was about eleven. I was introduced to pornography as a teen growing up. I was taught from my peers that pornography and masturbation was the norm and that it was okay. Porn and masturbation, or P&M was literally everything to me. Whenever I felt down and out, depressed, or sometimes just idle in my time I would always turn to P & M. I didn't realize the severity of my actions until after I got married however. It was literally during the last two years that I started to see just how strong this beast had become. Every time the going got tough and I felt like a failure as a husband or that I could never be the man that I envisioned, I would turn to my beast for satisfaction. Trying to start a career or your own business can be very tough and for me it was. I had so many dreams about what could be, but I was constantly plagued, by what wasn't happening and the depressing feeling that I would never make it.

However, I wasn't aware that every time something got hard or began to be a little too much for me, I would go to what I knew. Like I said, I had grown up with it for so long, it felt like the norm to me. The issue here is that I was taking my worries about my situation back to the source of my problem. Instead of talking things out with my wife or using positive forms of affirmation, I'd feel more comfortable watching another woman that I had absolutely no connection to. Feeling like she would give me a sense of peace from what I was dealing with, but by the end I was always feeling bad about what I had done. I would constantly allow myself and my marriage to be poisoned by my lack of control over my desires which prevented me from being able to see the bigger picture, and kept me from recognizing exactly where I was wasting my idle time.

I was allowing a cycle to be created that I couldn't shake and didn't know why until I realized that I kept feeding my beast every time I allowed my mind to wander off into this fantasy world; just to get away from my problems. Sometimes we can be totally unaware of what we are really allowing to happen during that moment because our minds are wondering away from the problem at hand rather than the figuring out a productive solution. The solution to you overcoming whatever your beast lies in your commitment to yourself, your dream and your future.

Therefore, in order for you to be fully committed to yourself, you have to make a commitment to starving your beast that may or may not be present right now. When we think of the word commitment it is typical for our minds to resort to a relationship of some sort. The same kind of commitment that you put into letting that beast back in is the same type of commitment you have to put into yourself. I knew how my beast had such a strong hold on me and even though I felt guilty every time I got involved with it; I couldn't help but to open myself up again. This was the case until January of 2014. I had to make the decision on what was more important: my love for my wife and my future or the urge to feed the never ending beast that latched on to me. This would seem like a no brainer to many, but the truth is that it wasn't. It was hard for me to let go of something that I had been attached to for so long. And even though my beast wasn't a true comfort, it felt enough like comfort to the point I wanted it to stay with me. But I knew that I couldn't live a lie anymore, until I was put in a position where I had to choose. Even though my beast had been a cycle in my life for so long, I constantly remind myself that I made a promise to my wife when I said "I Do."

Ask yourself the same thing. "What do I really want to be committed to?" Which of these can I afford to sacrifice in order to fulfill what I was destined to do? The one thing I do know is that your commitment to yourself and your goals has to outweigh the commitment that you have with that beast that is your distraction. Here is some insightful truth for you. Your beast could literally live with you forever, giving you comfort every time something doesn't go right, and could possibly grow into an addiction. That possible addiction could knock you off your course and hinder you from succeeding in life. With that being said, is it worth risking or can you afford to lose the distraction in order to make the life you wish to have a reality? COMMIT TO STARVING THE BEAST

Chapter 10: The Leap

"Faith is taking the first step even when you don't see the whole staircase."
– Dr. Martin Luther King Jr.

The process of building your faith can bring a person so many uncertainties. It's like when you first have the vision and you see yourself doing something so amazing, it's all fine and dandy. But as soon as you step into the process that leads to your promise, boom, everything you once believed in comes into question. You may begin to ask, "Am I really good enough? Is this journey really for me? Maybe I'm in over my head." All of a sudden, things are not as certain as they once seem. Or at least that's what we are supposed to believe. When you start believing in that which you are passionate about you will be tested like you could never imagine. While it seems unfair, this is necessary to build character and strength. You might ask, "Why do I need character and strength? I already have that, so what's the point?" This might be true, but for the level of greatness you are headed to, you will need more than what you already have. You can't expect to walk into greater levels or a higher purpose, with the same gear you have on now. The process of faith, belief and hope is really a process to test the guts and balls we say we have and to give us the ones we need.

I'm reminded of a good friend of mine who played professional football. This guy was a highly scouted athlete coming out of high school and college. A lot of prospects knew that he was talented and arguably one of the best players in his draft class. He knew it too and he was just happy that his hard work finally paid off and got him into the NFL. When he got drafted, he was ready, but something was different about him. He seemed a little more relaxed; a little too relaxed to me. He went into the first day of training camp playing with the 3rd string and special teams unit. He called me after the first day in a panic. He said to me "Rich, I didn't sign up for all of this." I asked him what he meant and he goes on to tell me that the speed of the game is different, the players are stronger and he was heated about starting from the bottom of the roster.

He lashed out and said, "I'm a draft pick with talent and I've proven myself over and over again. This is not what I imagined after having to go through hell just to get here." At that very moment it became very clear to me. He was under the impression that because he had a vision and put in the hard work to make it to draft day with a nice salary, that this was it. I had to calm him down and explain to him that he could not expect the work that he's done before the NFL to carry him through a successful professional career.

In order for him to see his full potential he would have to understand that his process is not yet complete. This is the same mindset we need to have when we begin taking our own "Leap of Faith" and proactively move towards greater things. We have to know in our mind that the road gets hard and promises will be broken. Jobs might be lost, business deals with great potential may fall through our hands, but know that just because you put in a great amount of hard work to make that dream a reality, doesn't mean you will be fully validated when you reach your goal.

Complacency is a friend of hindrance and it will suck you in without warning. If you are looking to be successful in your leap of faith, you must keep a fire for consistent execution. This will be your guiding light when you reflect on what you have accomplished already. The key is not getting overwhelmed or overly confident with the things that you've done, because there is and always will be room for improvements. My principle for you to take is this: Don't flaunt average or good as though it is greatness. Until you die there can always be new things to achieve.

When you are functioning in your faith you must remember that you do not need to defend your dream or fight those that do not share your conviction. Too many times we get caught up trying to defend our decisions and the things that we want to do with our life. Your family and friends, and even unwarranted strangers will try to break down your reasoning for why you are making the choices that you choose to make. Understand, that they are not trying to tear you apart or make you feel less than. Before you try to defend that last statement, hear me out.

Our natural instinct is to think from a literal or realistic way of thinking. Everything has to make perfect logical sense, according to our own reasoning, or it doesn't make sense at all. But remember, that's what faith is all about; believing in something, without being able to physically see it at the time and without it making sense to anyone but you. When your journey gets tough and people doubt you, your focus has to be on building up your faith in yourself and your dreams. There are three steps I want you to take in order to build your faith. They are feeding your faith, refuse to accept doubt, and act on your faith.

In chapter nine I discussed the idea of starving the beast that can keep us hindered. I purposely starve my beast, because every time we give in to it, we are feeding it again. So I also want to remind you to convert your energy into things that matter. Begin to feed your faith the same way you have been feeding your beast. A few ways you can feed your faith are through prayer, meditation, reading literature on having faith and also being around people who will keep you uplifted and encouraged. Being around or in contact with people who can help influence your faith is an invaluable tool. For example, I am constantly inspired and fed through the help and support of everyone that supports my work, whether online, in person, or however we engage. Every time I have a conversation with someone about how my stories of life have affected them, my faith is being fed. There are times when I get weary, and I will receive a random text or message from someone I have known for a while, or someone who has stumbled across my work. Those messages mean so much. They show me that taking a leap of faith is actually making an impact in someone else's life; which in turn gives me more faith to keep going.

I encourage you to be mindful of people around you that are genuinely building up your faith. Refuse to accept doubt; whether doubting yourself or if someone doubts you. It is natural to have negative thoughts that surface from time to time. But just because thoughts of doubt surface, doesn't mean we have to accept them as our reality. When you do, it's almost like saying, "I give you permission to step into my space and make me feel differently about myself than what I should." Remember, you don't have to allow anything to take over your thoughts, because you are the gatekeeper of your brain. Instead accept great possibilities, seek great thoughts, and don't accept doubt. When you find yourself contemplating doubt, evaluate it. Find one thing that you know to be true about yourself, which cannot be disproved, and use that to reject the notion that the doubtful thoughts could ever be true.

Finally, you must act on your faith. When I say act on your faith, I mean putting action behind what you believe in. If there is an opportunity presenting itself to you, jump on it. Don't be afraid of the outcome, just act. If you don't reach your goal, it's okay. A great part of your success will come from your failures. Michael Jordan shared with the world how he missed more than 9,000 shots throughout his career, lost 300 games and has missed the winning game shot 26 times. He is quoted saying, "I've failed over and over again in life, and that's why I succeed." I believe that Michael Jordan understood that in order to have immense success, you have to increase your failure rate. You have to be willing to hear some "no's" and make mistakes, while maintaining your faith. We will never be perfect in our percentage of success, and we don't need to be. Your focus should be on taking the leap. Examine where you failed and capitalize on those failures by strengthening those areas that caused you to fail in the first place. Is there an area you feel like you can afford to take a leap of faith in? Are there doubts that you need to block from your thoughts? Take some time to think about the people in your life that help you feed your faith, and see how you can be more intentional about your encounters with them. The cool thing about the leap is that while you can't always control the direction while in midair, you can always focus on executing a clean landing. So, don't be afraid… Take the leap.

Chapter 11: What's in Your Hands?

"What does love look like? It has the hands to help others. It has the feet to hasten to the poor and needy. It has eyes to see misery and want. It has the ears to hear the sighs and sorrows of men. That is what love looks like."
                                    –Saint Augustine

What's in your hands? This is a question that was asked by the late Adam Clayton Powell Jr. In 1968 during what most would consider his best speech ever, Dr. Powell was speaking directly to the impoverished 18th district of New York and it was a call to action. The people of Harlem were struggling hard with 30% of the population unemployed. The people complained to him about how they weren't like him. They weren't congressmen who were making a little money. They didn't have the same luxuries that they assumed he had. What I love about his speech was that he was trying to get the people to understand not only the power of choice, but the fact that they control the power of choice as well. After hearing the people state every power that they didn't have, Dr. Powell responded by telling them that they have the power of choice. Dr. Powell used some great examples to bring his point to life. He reflected on the story of Moses, who had a speech impediment and only a stick, but still had the power to lead his people to the Promised Land. He spoke of George Washington Carver who was so frail he was traded for a broken down home as a slave. However, Carver was the same individual who revolutionized peanuts, cotton, and the sweet potato for the entire world. And also Ben Franklin who had a string and a kite, that was struck by lightning, leading to his work with creating electricity. So, what's in your hands? I could go on for days with great stories of people who had what most would consider as nothing, but were able to take that "nothing" and create something that added value to their life and the life of others.

Despite your upbringing, background, or mistakes; the question still remains, "What's in your hands?" Don't take for granted the power you possess. If you can be bold enough to stretch your hands out and believe in yourself, then the power inside of you will morph into greatness. Anything that you want in life is possible. It is up to you to get to the point where you realize that your power is stronger and more important than the opposition you face. I've said this in several chapters, but I will tell you one final time, THE WORLD NEEDS YOU!

The reason why I'm asking you what's in your hands is because your hands are a representation of your journey. So it is time for you to pick up where you left off. Correct the mistakes you've made in the past and realize that they only still linger because you allow them to. I don't care if you completely walked away and turned your back on your dreams, or if you've hit a stumbling block and can't seem to get up. You have the power to get up, keep going, create and produce things that the world has never seen. Change does not start with the people that we vote into office or what the media glorifies. Change starts within us, it always has. I believe that we have been taught to believe otherwise at times, but there is still no need to doubt. I believe that you were created with a purpose and plan that can only be completed by you.

This book has focused a lot around dealing with some real deep issues that you may be facing or have faced in the past. The reason behind this is because a lot of successful people talk about their success from a before and after stand point, never really stressing the process that it took to get to a successful end. However, I believe that if we start to discuss our processes in depth, we can really help others and ourselves. It can remind us of what we have overcome and give us hope to realize how much more we can overcome. I encourage you not to be afraid of showing others what to expect and how to avoid certain challenges during their similar process. I say similar because you may encounter someone who thinks, acts, and shares some of the same experiences as you. We were all created to impact specific people in our life and we can do that by recognizing and using what's in our hands. Your journey has the potential to be the guiding path for some desperate soul to avoid the same mistakes and also capitalize on what could be missed opportunities. I don't want you to ever think that the bumps and bruises you have experienced through your journey have been for nothing. Take selfish thoughts out of the equation. A lot of times we can tend to think from a "woe is me" mentality, but you have to remember that you are choosing to take this process on, because of your belief that it will change your life and potentially the life of someone else.

But before you get to that point, you have to embrace that journey and find your purpose from it. This journey is not just about becoming the next big thing in your respective fields. Your journey is also about giving hope to people that could have been another statistic of greed, depression, suicide, homicide, homelessness and so on. The experiences that lay in your hands will birth life, but only if you take the time to reflect on what's in your hands.

My hope is that you find the value in the power you already possess while embracing this tough process to accomplishing your dreams. When times get tough and you begin to question the purpose of chasing your goals and accomplishing your dreams, remind yourself that you were never meant to fail. And the only time that you can fail is when you decide to stop using what's in your hands. One thing I have learned throughout my own personal process is to constantly remind myself that leaders are birthed out of times of adversity. So while things seemed like they were getting worst around me, what was really happening is that my process was preparing me to be the cure, the hope and the change for those who can't see life past their current day. I might not know you personally and maybe we have never met, but the fact that you are reading this book is an example of me using what's in my hands. Your choice to give my work a chance is what helps me fight off my own inadequacy, pushes me to take more leaps and ultimately keeps me motivated while I'm waiting on my next moment. The same way you impact me, is the same way that you can impact the people around you and they will ultimately go and impact others. This is what I consider global impact, and it all started from you figuring out and using what's in your hands. You don't need to do anything extravagant, just accept your journey for what it is and use what's already in your hands to make your dreams and goals a reality. By doing this, you make the possibility of success more realistic for those around you through encouragement. This is the power that rest behind the greatness and capability in your hands.

Author's Bio

With his big smile and even bigger personality, Richard Taylor hails from Chicago, IL. Growing up on the Southeast Side of Chicago, Richard was exposed to a number of unsettling issues in his youth; but he remained focused and maintained his stance as a positive influence for his peers. Richard dealt with insecurity, low self-esteem, and feelings of worthlessness that resulted from being bullied and ridiculed in his childhood. These issues followed him into young adulthood and later contributed to self-destructive behavior.

Now at the age of 26, Richard Taylor is a nationally recognized best-selling author and speaker. He is on a mission to be one of the influential voices for his generation and the generations to come. His high-energy, motivational YouTube series "Getting Over The Hump" and debut book *Unashamed* have quickly positioned him as one of the fastest growing speakers in the market. In a short time Richard has been able to share the stage with Pioneers, Celebrities and Global Philanthropist such as Isaiah Thomas, Star Jones, Founder of Global Grind. Michael Skolnik and CNN Contributor and Founder of Rebuild The Dream, Van Jones. Richard's story of overcoming morbid obesity, depression, suicide, failing in college and domestic abuse, has struck a change within people throughout the country. Richard inspires the masses to tap into their inner potential to create the change they want to see.

Richard L. Taylor Jr.
Author, Speaker & Consultant

Contact
contact@unashamednation.com

Visit My New Website
www.unashamednation.com

23546644R00064

Made in the USA
Columbia, SC
13 August 2018